Paddy Lambe's in Paradise

for Emer Mary Charlotte Rose

John McGuckian

Paddy Lambe's in Paradise

ARLEN
HOUSE

Paddy Lambe's in Paradise

is published in 2019 by
ARLEN HOUSE
42 Grange Abbey Road
Baldoyle
Dublin 13
Ireland
Phone: 00 353 86 8360236
arlenhouse@gmail.com
arlenhouse.blogspot.com

978–1–85132–214–5, *paperback*

Distributed internationally by
SYRACUSE UNIVERSITY PRESS
621 Skytop Road, Suite 110
Syracuse
NY 13244–5290
Phone: 315–443–5534
Fax: 315–443–5545
supress@syr.edu
syracuseuniversitypress.syr.edu

cover images are reproduced courtesy of
Dr Hugh McGuckian

LOTTERY FUNDED

Contents

III PARADISE

'Was you thinking at all of poetry?' Mr Wegg inquired, musing.

'Would it come dearer?' Mr Boffin asked.

'It would come dearer,' Mr Wegg returned. 'For when a person comes to grind off poetry night after night, it is but right he should expect to be paid for its weakening effect on his mind.'

– Charles Dickens, *Our Mutual Friend*

I

Dinn's Inn

PADDY LAMBE'S IN PARADISE (1971)

I remember we had a couple of pints each
in Paddy Lambe's –
though Eoiny Goat hit the orange
laced with Pernod – an' another wee drink
in Dinn's Inn at Ballyhackamore –
before descending on Joe's party
on down the Upper Newtownards Road.

The craic had been about Beetles –
my 1303s with its double back-axle,
Eoiny's '62 1200 – about keeping late hours
and making heavy weather of the violent
scenes in East Belfast. Eoiny had turned
his pioneer pin in, thinking of Down Under.

The party was wild, Joe's compensation money
having come through a couple of days before –
they were handing out great mugs of vodka
laced with poitin from the hallstand.

A variety of girls had been imported, though
Joe's wee daughters started the jiving. I
walked in on Joe taking the knickers off
a sizeable blonde and slipped back
among the madness all around – they were
intent on spending the £85,000 all in one
evening, and though the food wasn't so good,
the booze was drunk like there was no tomorrow.

Eoiny was jumping through the low-bay
front-window, chasing the girls round the garden –
teenagers, furious with strong liquor, were ripping
their clothes off, feeling totally in love, jiving
up and down the hall-stairs.

I remember I took a notion to go home –
we had ended up sadly, three or four mates in a bed
staring at the ceiling –
and the Beetle flying up the Newtownards Road
at seventy-miles-an-hour in third gear

and then the motorway roundabout at Ballymena
hit me three times before I stopped short
of the drop over the side.

Joe had been hit by a bullet in the spine
at the Kennedy Way roundabout;
paralysed from the waist down,
he was sent to Stoke-Mandeville.

And I was sitting at the Pennybridge,
outside Ballymena, thinking that I could easily
be full of lead instead.

Top o' the Mornin', Father (1971)

My Lochaniuir Under-Fifteens would have barely
survived against Malachy's,
would have been heading out the gates to meet
live rounds bouncing down from Lynch's pub.

Gerard Hagan, centre-back, that barely attended
College but mysteriously appeared for matches,
would declare he was already late for his Saturday job –
so I would have swung my white Transit towards the Circus,
praying like Father Charlie Agnew who couldn't see
a stime that Our Lady would protect his blue Beetle.

Jesus, I probably thought, this is my family van and
the bloody President would be sitting out in his safe house
munching his way through pounds of French apples –
the same boyo that advised a female member of his staff
that brillo-pads were provided in the ladies' loo
wouldn't have been too keen to have invested
in a bullet-proof vehicle for the college team.

Fuck this, I would have said into myself, for a lark.

Downview 1980s

A neighbour's eldest son
would have whispered to me:
They're clicking-in live rounds!
The two of us crouching there
at the junction of Downview with Innisfayle.

There would have been another bomb
in the Golf Club – a possible attack on the judge
who'd scored well over par, probably, that Wednesday.
Us, wondering should we hit the dust,
like the caretaker taught us – he that had
fought down in Gallipoli and had played –
he would have insisted – to a handicap of six
at Mahee Island well before his sister died.

Those boys would have been cool as ice,
I'm telling you, ready for action – but
it would have been squeezy-bum time
for civilians, children, mice, wondering if this
would be the last view they'd have of the County Down.

DANDY STREET
(Nov. 1994)

In this sort of war,
Jesus asks for sandwiches
between Chichester and the Boundary Bar.

'Have a go at the Lotto', my children cry
as I obediently pull in at Greencastle,
two Californian lilacs having caught my eye

at Maisiey's vegetable shop that's up for sale
in some kind of ultimate depression
that the 'Greenweeds' can't survive the pale.

I fly on along the Shore Road, eye my fold,
swerve through a tangle of Mass-goers
crossing a motorway-entrance tinged with gold.

Litter is hanging from every bush, every tree,
as Church Militant dander from altar to home
certain whose spirit lays claim to the land of the free.

'Sold-out' their mural reads as we flash by,
heading for our bolt-hole in Tir-na-nOg .
We, like refugees crossing the Elbe, can now fly,

for cruxed as they are between Boundary and Star,
we can stop at the oasis of Old Tannaghmore
to make sure this little army is well fed in its car!

In the Queue

She was all Sixties; would have been
at the Troxy Cinema
the first time we queued there
for 'Naked as Nature Intended'.

Today at the post-office counter,
she couldn't find the card-holder,
never mind her pin number or
'How to Put It In'.

'He'll kill me', she splutters, 'it's his card –'
in the queue, in my eagerness to help,
I grazed a second lady's fingers –
'Much to Her Delight'.

'I thought I'd touched', this old girl says,
half-turning in her agony.
'I suppose you're disappointed –'
'Not at all, no way'.

'I've had one or two', the first lady says,
but the post-mistress smiles:
'Just shove it in there' – 'An' join the queue',
my friend prays, as we break into stitches!

Our Wee Girl
(couldn't be fifty; no way Jose)

'England', he said, 'is in storage'.
This in the Titanic Quarter.
I suppose if your doting aunt lives in Blacklion
and you're unsure what you're going to say
to the old dearo – well, maybe 'storage'.

He was at Bernadette's Party – dare I say
her fiftieth: unbelievable the life force
in that girl; hopping around the Blue Star Line's
floor like a young Russian peasant on the boards.
And with a young Bishop in tow, to boot.

At the Pump House our hearts sank –
mein gott in himmel but the cold breeze
from off the Cavehill left us near paralysed –
and then I thought of his old aunt, and took off
my hat, not wanting to look a right little softee.

It was a scene right out of William Trevor:
The Big Farmer to my left at the dinner table
owned an 8000 acre farm in the wilds of Tyrone,
and could smell a Taig a mile off – my wee mind
working overtime of course on the Herdman.

Bernadette's sister was on stage, singing.
I thought I could be her manager: she would
easily make it as a country-and-western star.
We were all getting tipsy in the Trident port and
the lonely old mother refused to dance with me.

I'd sunk three bottles of the Piceno, the dark
Italian vino that makes you think you're Al Pacino.
The Farmer's Wife did dance – well, I jumped up

and down like Mick Jagger and she, with her
dystrophy, tried to move her head vertically.

A rum crew. A strange lot. Black beef after finger
prawns. The Italian husband leaned further back,
his sons casually playing pool at a safe distance.
The English Blonde was saying she grew up in a graveyard.
Jesus, some of us grew up in a cemetery called Belfast.

It's still our wee country. All we've got. Still,
why did she return from Moscow to this snow?
This slight drift; this cold damp air off the lough?
To give us a lift? Cheer us up. Say thanks. After all
we brought her up to be a real cracker!

THE QUICK-MAN

Do you know him?
Nobody knows him.
Probably stocious.

He's full-drunk.

I don't think he's been drinking.
Just bloody sad, my daughter says.

'I'm subject to seizures' –
Billy raises his head, momentarily,
from the cold ground near Seaview.

He's still breathin'.

He's out of a home.
Look at them clothes.

I smelt his breath.
His eyes is flickerin'.
His head's all blood.

He's a nobody.

His shirt is tucked in.
No way he's a drunk, my daughter says.

The Quick-Doctor feels for a pulse.
I'm a doctor, he says. Walks back
to the Quick-Car. The Quick-man smiles too.

It's Billy. We know him.

My Volvo is blocking the Massive Truck.
The daughter is still briefing the Royal.

The Big Ambulance arrives.
A crowd of locals gathered at the bottom of Downview.
Jesus! That's quick, my daughter says.

It's only Billy Foster.

Bleeding on the cold, cold ground.
Six passers-by upset.

The Quick-Man's slapping him.
He's slappin' him too hard, my
daughter cries.
Billy, Billy, come on now son!

He's slapping Billy on the cheek.
Knows him!

PATHFINDER

How can I walk along the rue St Denis
and not regard it as a billiard green
for Il Long Carabine.
I mean that big blonde
in the black crude under-leather
may eat her baguette out defiantly
And the Exterminator of Rats, Voles and Vermin,
display stuffed corpses –
but I say look at that poor rat with a twisted foot!
or yon mink caught in the limo'!

So French the big chimney breasts,
black slates, high slants,
flower-baskets competing for space!
Our own Lone-Walker would have collected
here for animal rights, but what competition
from the professional soldiers of rue Etienne Marcel!

Everywhere the ancient ritual must be done:
An old lady in René Vallinay Parc sets up
for lunch only to move on again quickly;
From the Pont Neuf boats carry lovers;
at Shakespeare & Co., Prospero has a late brunch.

In a side-chapel of Notre-Dame, a young priest
hears the sins of a first-class blonde:
In the cool darkness, everyone is beautiful.
Even my Protestant friends brave ancient
antipathies for my sake.
When all is said and done, confession
becomes a conversation beneath blue.

Graffiti Parisienne

Jock has a dander round St Honoré with Maigret

M. Beneath Cluny's ancient walls the sun-dial
wears an ancient badge of lamp-shells,
a mosaic from 1212 A.D.; its shingle
reads: *Nil Sine Nobis.*

J. 'No Surrender' if my O-level Latin serves
me well; 'Jock McNinch' might be closer still.

M. At the well-curb the schoolboy spits his soul
into the darkness to set it free.
Mon dieu, here on the rue Hautefeuille:
Ninth of April, 1821, Charles Baudelaire –
La Maison Ou Nequit.

J. You'd need to get your finger out
in Belfast to find Heaney's old house.

M. For the sake of Parisienne traffic, skirts
split down the back; taxis wear red, white and blue.

J. Look at this beside the video bins: 'Mother
fuckin noise': beats 'Prods Out' or 'No Irish'.

M. In Paris we have many blues: coupe water
Lily bleu or Vase Nymphale bleu or
a sere-sucker dress at f632.

J. We make do with Royal Blue – seriously though,
yesterday my friend and I were the only ones
to stand in from the rain: our Ulster notes not
legal tender though bullet-proof.

M. Notice how two sides of the same street
remain centuries apart: aspects of a face
in the Louvre, of Kate Barthelemy.

J. To be brutally honest, Inspector – though you
may have twigged on – we were hiding
from the Film-Maker, his imaginary friend having
killed herself as second in a Miss Ireland Competition.

RUE DANTON

a rattling boot,
a wooden shingle,
diamond peepholes –
night closing like
an Irish dawn

you are drawn
standing
back against this
ancient wall –
a small hotel,
St Honoré,
dream-time.

There is no rhyme
you say or reason
for such a separation.
My heart beats for you –
we have both heard
the tumbrils roar
along the same street.

We might meet
again someday –
I know you were in this room;
I'm not just dreaming or
maybe the truth is in the dream.
Its like the hidden message of
Obi Kenobi in the robot – you
thought of me strongly when
you dreamt here! Some great
power has meant your image
hits me in the self-same room
you slept in –

a student travelling in Paris,
for loves sake!

Cry & Pay

Near Le Carrousel de Louvre, Pyramide Inversée,
a little gypsy girl sleeps on the verge
just beyond the walls of Charles V,
her tiny feet tucked into themselves.

Model boats are pushed out with wooden sticks
on to the fish pond in the Tuleries,
their twin-sails patchworked with love and care;
carp gape and goldfish roam
among the caravelles of wondering daddies;
Pigeons hop up and down, envious.

A sneering group of gypsies organise themselves
with walky-talkies: has the child lain still,
still enough to make the tourist cry and pay?

I hear Emer's voice from over the waves –
she likes the fish, boats and happy pigeons –
'Daddy, can't you feel her pain?'

In the Commune

I felt at home in the parish hall –
just stepped up to her pelisse stall
and noticed her cheeks in bloom.

I could hear the rappels of the Commune –
wondered how the ancient band kept in tune
amidst that crepuscular gloom.

She wore ivy and gilly-flowers brand new
especially for la fete-Dieu –
a Kermis at the parish hall.

I thought she might have felt my joy
imagining I'd fought at Fontenoy –
her immortelles held me so in thrall.

Hard to find *la mot juste,* get close to you –
lighter than diamond your smile, but true
you hardly noticed me at all!

Whitestar League
Fröjel Churchyard

That breaker of earth, from Mulde;
This Chief justice from Alstade;
A soldier and his wife in their family
grave; a cottage – owner; grandmother
and grandson Olof; all together now,
a tiny white star before their birth-date,
a simple cross against their death.

Postcard from Visby

i

Marguerita sent me a card
from Visby. It showed buttresses,
portal doors, lowest socles – you
would think you were inside
the ancient walls.

She said her husband had grown
too old for travelling; that he
disliked new names; that he was
too old for unbelief; that he could
understand how sad I might be.

Snow fell anciently that year
in Visby: above the Cathedral,
over bulwarks, against buttresses,
portals, socles –
all broken hearts.

ii

Yet in the Spring, another letter
in my door. A Gotland name:
Ihre, it said, 'Ihre' quite plainly.
As if some birthright claimed
from the ancient dead.

Apparently – watching young people
repainting headstones – Marguerita's
husband had suddenly remembered:
We rented the house out in summertime!
To a student last time, name of Ihre.

But I may as well have lain down
among my own ancient dead.
No replies. The students had moved on.
Marguerita said she'd loved the letter
that I'd sent as if to my friend, Helmy.

iii

And then her letter came to Belfast,
just as I had agreed to publish the poems
I wrote in agony of love in the *Cork Review*.
'Do you remember me?' it asked. 'Do you
remember the hedgehog above the steps?'

She said she thought I was a German –
tourist you know – and laughed when
I told her I was a kind of poet, being Irish:
I was representing my own little country:
Northern Ireland.

It was an International Poetry Festival
and she could read my name on the list
of writers from round the world. We had tea
and held hands and walked through the
cobbled streets. And I kissed her cheek.

And really that was that.

FÅRÖ

Your pink toes feel among
a carpet of sand –
your eyes so deeply brown
the sunlight stared.

Along the medieval gold
of your eyelashes
a rare deep-blue Baltic shadow
fell far away

emperor and dark and light blue
songs fell from your slender body
into an island
of a thousand churches.

They told me later in my grief
that Faro was beautiful;
That I would forget you
as the days grow old.

Your black nipples under silk
and gold lie interwoven
with my dreams,
falling sunstar red dreams.

St Hansvarterens

Long ago in Öland,
by a grey sea,
low-angled waves lapped
the Baltic Shield.

Today, under that same skyline,
your pink toes clink
archaen pebbles, and you talk
of Viking Gold:
How Danish ships had anchored off,
their sea-eyes fixed
on samite cloths, medieval tapestries
in colours of the Kings of Spain;
How a beach-walker raised the alarm
whilst dreaming of red-limestone cliffs
in some warmer clime: send for Riddare Hans,
Hanskvarterens for Wisby!

You pictured me as an Irish shepherd boy,
gazing along warm green Antrim pastures –
I thought I might have been your Riddare Hans,
saving you and yours from empty dreams.

Swedish Sisters

i Helmy

To cheer her elder sister up –
save her from electric therapy –
she leaves cash items, little gifts
after all her pain of being mugged.

A woman's purse is sacred –
Sancta Maria the last resort;
even along a city's poorest road
you might find the Holy Family.

ii Edit

A rough autumnal storm rattles away
at the metal gutters: big drops
of rain make music. Sister's house
becomes a chocolate umbrella.

Eat cake; play games; read poetry
together. Fire with old wood;
Drink old wine; read old books.
Have old friends.

iii Helmy

See how the storm
brings us together.
How good lies at her heart.

The Moon over Oslo

What is this precious pearl
but the holy-water of your birth;
a mussel-shaped red limestone star,
sent from the Tsar to grandmother,
climbs higher and higher, almost
touching Laponia, her samite eyes
staring into the Russian snow.

You whisper to me that Gotland
is the island of wind-and-roses,
show me your little wooden house:
rosemary at the door, medieval
climbing roses, miniature yellow roses
like Viking boats at tiny windows.

You take my hand, ask me to return
someday –
I say that as the rose is the flower
of all flowers this the house
of all houses –
and if I were data I'd be there now.

Princess Grace's Irish Library

Imagine three girls
catching me out
between one translation and the other.

They thought I had escaped
from their Georgian bookcase –
the one securing Ulysses, first Paris edition.

This one's jaw dropped
at the wild Irish looks – who do you think
you are, George Bernard Shaw?

I'd just dandered round
from lighting a candle in the little
side-chapel of Mary of Perpetual Succour.

The girls suspected
I'd popped out of my own translation
of the *Annals*, on display on a side-table.

Some alter me had caught their eye –
can you not recognise a bloody ghost
when you see one, I said.

They regained their dignity easily enough;
Me, Connell of Lismoyne, Westmeath, left
lonely as a statue in the middle of Monaco.

The Sunny Spanish Shore

Swifts and swallows followed us
like Earls
beyond Biscay
into a sky weeping of Galician light –

light from a hidden sun
yellow, orange and red through the fog;
our boat like a stone scraping
a cottage-window moon in unknown mistiness.

At the instant of disappearance of the sun,
a green flash, a shooting flame, above
the high-treble of the surf, the mezzo-voice
of stones being dashed about –
imprisoned air boomed bass; the high-pitched
sound of sand in motion played a tune in ogham.

The girl spoke softly in Gallego;
like enshadowed pines her comrades, armed and
anxious to get on – the inn likely in its hiddenness.

Guitars played an ancient air; a boy sang a sentimental
song of how a father's love once given is eternal, a
mother's smile a light into eternity.

The girls danced till all our thoughts lifted
into one great swirl: McMahon abu!

To Ireland, take me home, my dear one sighed;
Mavourneen, little one, I prayed,
listen to the wild waves across a Celtic Sea:
home forever be's our stricken hearts!

VIA ANTRIM

Something of home
in the green-hills, the wavering
coastline of Galicia;
an inexpressible longing, an
emptiness more intense than the blues.

Something of home
in the sea-lands, a longing
for Antrim.

Sean could not translate
'humiliation' nor 'soul wounding',
translate the untranslatable;
even a friend might say *'se ve mal'* –
it is not looked on well, not in public.
He hid the books. Even at home
it had been a desolating attack.

Something of a sad land,
wounded in soul, inseparable
from a love of the nation;
something of a humiliated people,
disturbed and frustrated;
something of Rosalia de Castro,
Alfonso the Wise, even Garcia Lorca –
a few lyrics, songs to the Virgin,
an honoured life.

Something of home
in the green-hills, the wavering
coastline of Galicia;
some inexpressible longing
more intense than the blues.

Sean could not translate
the untranslatable: 'morrina' –
homesickness,
nostalgia,
emptiness of soul.

Something of home, though,
in the laughter of children, the wavering
coastline of Antrim.

SONS OF THUNDER

It was when I saw the names:
Hugh, Guillen and Maximo.
I thought they might have been
my own sons.

We were visiting Santiago de Compostela,
looking at names on granite pieces
in a Gothic cloister.

Guillen had been a master of railing
and watch maker; Hugh, Maestro
Mateo, builder; Maximo, artist.

They'd lived their mortal lives
along this medieval cloister –
all loved the French Road Door.

Santiago de Compostela had been
an ancient township once – like
Dunaghy, Carey or Dunloy.

And my fine sons might have been
happy here amongst the Celts:
Sons of thunder.

I think, though, the roles might
need rearranging: Liam, the builder;
Hugh, the artist; Fergus, the watch-maker.

They're pilgrims here in Galicia,
paying tribute to the Portico of Glory,
wondering at the Roman foundations.

They might have lived their mortal lives
along this medieval cloister: might have
loved the Pax Romana, in their way.

Locus Sancti Jacobi
Santiago de Compostela

In the Crypt,
deep down, beneath the Portico of Glory,
three Limoges Crosses stand proud –
I wondered at them, wandered on,
came back to look again; again
came back; behind their glass protection –
I stood too.

Two smaller crucifixes at either side –
the large on in the middle, the one
with the awful crack in its left arm,
moved sideways, moved again.

Against my shoulder, a warm chin:
'The cross moved', her voice said,
and I, back in this mortal life,
should recognise that voice.

II

ALL SAINTS

Chronotherapy
(1949–1959)

Wilbert and I followed him up Hill Street
through Fairhill.
Full of wonder at the colours spied between
railings at The Clock:
Our first football match, nearly the end
for Belfast Celtic,
the beginning of a life-story's tick-tock for Jock.

Ten years later he made us corncrakes out of
a fine piece of beech –
it was serious. The Sky Blues were facing
Linfield in the Final.
Ella and Ethel spun woollen dollies while
'Tempus Fugit'
said his old favourite Wag-at-The-Wall.

We spent hours in the Goods Yard, marvelling
at the shunting wagons:
Scottish steel and Ulster workmanship in a
powerful combo of noise:
He lit a Willie Woodbine; complained of his back;
Worried a lot about
ever repairing that majestic 'Grandfather', or
regaining his old poise.

When the Twelfth came 'round, he forgot about
his bad back,
insisting I try on his Sash, smiling at my
blushing cheeks –
shaved and dressed up like a prince, happy
in his memories:
Showing true colours for a couple of weeks.

He was a good, kind neighbour; loved his children;
Fought for his rights:
Swore he would take his back to 'higher
Authority!'
When I broke his kitchen-window with a ball,
he retired to his clocks;
'Time will tell', he thought, 'if he's another
Jimmy McGhee!'

The State Picture-House

We were all lined up for the matinee
outside the State Picture-House,
the Pogue twins prancing up and down
asking what time it was and though nobody
had a watch we knew there was a brave while
before the side-door opened and we could pour
in to see Hoppalong Cassidy and the Three Stooges.
'It'ill no tak Sammy an' me long to wait
half-an-hour' was bold Jimmy's reply.
'You'll jiggle the stations', Sammy said
looking at the wet-wireless batteries.
The whole row laughed in glee, clinking their
jam-jars down the sloping floor to the desk
and on inside to the warm-dark picture-house.

The excitement was furious when our hero
and his side-kick Gabby Hayes appeared on the
scene: black & white on the silver screen
an' very little 'talkin bits' or kissing to spoil
the Western action. It was a good show and
on the Trailer were Johnny MackBrown and
    the Cisco Kid.
I was sharing a quarter of clove rocks with my
sisters and kept a vice-grip on two-ounces
of teacakes sticking to paper. The film broke down
to howls of delight and our necks were stiff craning
up from the very front stalls at the wee projection
window and its beam of cigarette smoke.

I was riding home by the Layde slapping my horse
on in drawls towards Duke Street when I spotted
the Golls and their gang near the Dispensary: I
hit the wall and fell over into the river and waded my
horse through the rapids, tying-up at the fence in

friendly territory near the Dummy Bamber's
garden shed, to reconnoitre.
It wouldn't take me long to wait half-an-hour!

The Sunday Dispatch

I was scanning the newspaper headlines
at O'Neill's Corner, fascinating
over titles: *The Reynold's News,*
The Chronicle, The People, The Graphic,
The Empire News; happy
as a ten-year-old could be, dandering
round his domain, peering in shop-windows,
in that peace that descended
of a Sunday morning.

I was half thinking of scouting on down
by Salisbury Square for the Gordons
sold the papers there, though Eva
always looked so sad and my face
reddened even then that she had
overheard me once thinking out loud:
'There's Sunshine Anne'.

Suddenly, at the bottom of Springwell Street
close to the Fountain Bar, one of the O'Neills
threw a brilliant short left-hook
at a big gypsy fellow and all hell broke loose:
three tinkers had Big Tam surrounded, then
one of the gang let a terrible gowl an' a yell
out of him when Tam broke his crown
with a shovel and the blood splattered
all over *The People*.

I ran home in shock to report the news,
having saved the money but paying the price
all the same.

Even in a Lean-to of Branches

i

Strange, isn't it, life;
Who would believe it?
When does a poem end?

She had been knocking
at my sister's door, at the same time
(mark you) as I was looking at her,

not having seen her since 1952,
in an old black and white photograph:
nice of her to be searching for my book,

the one I mentioned her granny in-
actually I named her family five times,
so this is the poem I wrote, for her really,

though maybe my sister that died young
is responsible; after all she's sitting beside
Dinky, in the photograph, on our window-sill,

thinking it might be time for some kind of move!

ii

her hair bleached at the sun temples;
finger-nails glinting like mother-of-pearl;
a white streak of petticoats flashing

at the bottom of her skirt; those Jewish features:
just a girl shot on a Brownie. Though
shadows from the Kodak are blue,

maybe darker with age; maybe
her eyes are darker now – she would
have grown womanly! Oh dearest child,

surely those are the blue borders of a little blouse;
those the vividly blue shadows of snow;
that a tiny cap of blue squirrel

that there is no noise, even muffled, in this old photograph,
only lends a gentle nostalgia, expelling all other thoughts,
other sensations, expressed as perfect silence;

yet those are narrow pitch-black eyes, squinting
like a blind person, and speaking to me;
as though a greenish thread-like line of moonlight-

rising in the imagination of an old man – illuminates
one corner; breaks the flow of the age's custom:
live (it says) with the heart's chosen,

even if on a window-sill, in the post-war euphoria!

Sheila's Cottage

i

It would have been a sunny day –
I mean my mum wouldn't have sent me
on the Carnlough Bus otherwise.
I would always be the same age –
between eight and ten – (even now
in my old age, in my mind).

McCombe's barking dogs and nipping geese
would be avoided at speed along a loanen
that was both wonderful and frightening.
I would often feel as brave as a knight on
approach to my aunt's little cottage.
I had eight cousins to play with: great riches.

I would be shy enough about bathing in
the Devenagh Burn, preferring to watch
the dragonflies. There was a deep well too –
open and dangerous – but a lilac tree hung
close and friendly over its side.

We would play Cowboys and Indians among
the bushes and branches and hens and ducks.
Aunt Sheila finally would us in for supper:
To syrup on freshly baked soda, and strong tea.
It would soon be time to wash up with Lifebuoy in the
little basin of pale blue enamel under an old cracked mirror.

ii

Once the spell was broken: my aunt's edgy sister
slapped me on the face. I would always go back
in my mind to Sheila's Cottage. To my aunt's
gentle smile. To the run along the loanen to catch

the Ballymena 'bus. To the Devenagh Burn and trees
and fields. Not allowing her to break
the quick of my soul.

All Saints

Every face, even our name
– slanting wildly towards Broughshane.
It was long ago, in a wind off Slemish
– McAuley's Field at Caugherty.
Would we ever see their likes again
– the lily whites, shamrocks emblazoned?
Elders longed for their youth, then
– beneath Dunnyvadden's ancient rath.
O'Neill, Quinn, Loughran and Agnew
– all hell broke loose in fearful memory.
McCambridge, O'Hara, Vaughan and O'Connell
– a priest had torn off his holy gear.
Alec Darragh seemed to be praying along the line
– war had been declared as for the dead.

It was a cow-patch, thistles full of pride
– would they ever see our likes again?
Then the Celtic drum of old, so true
– Aontroim Abú! Bailemeanagh slú!
A deep pulse, a lament for something of our own
– the Gentry riding out from beneath the rath!
It wasn't just Belfast Johnnies faced us then
– more the ancient, youthful eyes of Them!

The team stripped at the side of old Crebilly Road
– no hint of shelter from the lively Slemish wind.
Elders, priests, schoolmasters, parishioners in a ring
– would we ever see their likes again?
Bhí an lá sin fadó ó sóin
– ach is fada go gciúnoidh an racán!

Lis Ané

She could read my thoughts –
was it the Latin that I'd lost,
or some other?

My niece laughed at my liking
of that woman –
thunder thighs, she sneered.

And how can I speak that
have lost my tongue; even
to defend an ancient smile?

These country people have held
on to the Old Faith – to their
poor land too.

She might have snagged me –
might have enthralled me –
I hadn't the words to stay.

SPINNET

Near Altidore,
two hundred years of greening
grass, hooves holding
a long glenside lane,
shadows angling in her stream.

Near Altidore,
two great windows admiring
the very outline of that dress,
a rustling spinnet, old gates
creaking open, their tiny crown
rusting, tilting.

Near Altidore,
two legs drawn too straight,
the faces square, the boots right,
high collars in Napoleonic style.
poison for breakfast.

Near Altidore,
two hearts cracked, both
souls falling into the same
cloud above the Irish Sea.

Near Altidore,
two masks, one the appearance
of a mask, a shamrocked
seal in rustless gold, in a cabinet.

TEAMPAILLÍN BÁN
Lios Tuathail

Black slabs, flat like quartered malachite, their veins
like rings of a child's life – not your upright headstones
of the modern cemetery; no names or dates, nor any
little star, nor any sign or Christian salutation.

A large field; a mown perimeter walk; shrubs and bushes
flowering amongst the Stations of the Cross;
an old black metal crucifix on a white gate, and white
posts like candles everywhere.

According to the workhouse records – three thousand souls
a little chapel with pews and altar –
rosaries on plastic and wooden images
of The Virgin, St Anthony, Padre Pio etc.

I could still feel the raised earth beneath my teenage feet:
potato drills in the Braid; war-time flax-mounds along
the fifteenth at Fortwilliam Golf Course; the paupers
graves behind the Waveney Hospital Workhouse.

According to the workhouse records ... under fifteen years
of age.

LOCAL GEOLOGY

Yon Virgin's open arms,
her grotto;
tumbling over
of her small mountain stream-
over and over and out
of the Old Red Sandstone of
West Cork –
feelings of nowhere
true to go, the sudden snow.

Crank the 'phone: Ballingeary 3,
reverse charges northwards free.
sweet Belfast.

A late rush for Baile Bhuí
and the sea
over Antrim Basalt.

The Tower Centre Ballymena
after Máirtín Ó Direáin

I find solace for a brief spell
among thoughts of my own people.

I walk by Springwell, Ball Alley,
returning from the city.

I like the old faces I meet betimes
on the rounds in my mother's town.

I find solace for a while from sounds
of the city, sour voices of strangers.

It vexes my heart to think of those
not to be found in this shopping-centre.

Friends I had once, old flames, this
heated paradise our playground.

Thoughts are my real home now,
the old one bound as an island,

its impenetrable forest of shops,
its vegetation of business.

I find solace for a brief spell
among thoughts of my own people.

AUGUST

for Patsy

chill evening air
big drops of rain
Lammas Tide
threatening our freehold

some rebel gene
left over from the storm
beyond coalyard walls
deep trawling
yearning
pulse quickening

tribal feeling
without flag
without emblem

the tide alone or
a Month's Mind
may do

THE KICKING-HORSE KITCHEN

I thought it was just a dream –
but they said it could be your orb,
an emanation from a spiritual being.
I had been tinkering with my camera, right enough,
and they said they were being caught
more frequently these days by digital photography.

Bisto looked them up on Google:
Plasma-like transparent spheres, and, viewed
from a bar-stool, a sight to behold.
The front window of the Kicking-Horse was pure
Old-Ballycastle Glass. And if you looked closely
it was made up of sort of curvy, greeny, spheres.

But I said I would be turning a dream
into a nightmare if what I'd seen in the orb
was reported to the general public.
Maybe the Kicking-Horse Kitchen – strange name
for a pub anyway – was all a dream and the glass
orb thing a figment, but I recognised her face.

Never forget a face, was always me. Definitely
Rosie Raddie. Passed away these fifty years.
'I would have you know', she said, 'that Seven Dials
has changed a lot since our day'. Our day?
It was certainly a bar in Restoration London, in
Stuart Times. 'Go to the Dower House', she said,

'at Caugherty. The gate-house at Crebilly Castle.
There is a poor soul trapped there still – take pity!'
The priest had taken the right steps for exorcism.
He was a good man. Possessing a kind of innocence.
He said that it was only by very special diocesan
permission that such a ceremony could be allowed.

In these days, few believed in religion – the official
kind of stuff full of the old ritual.
Apparently, the bishop's aunt could have been
the poor soul's mother. She'd had to move
to London or face the nuns in the laundry
up the Ormeau Road in Belfast.

Fr O'Sullivan said the prayers in a quiet voice.
He sprinkled Holy Water over the doorposts.
I stood back against the outer front-window,
smoking, and wondering what would happen.
When I heard the old woman's voice, I knew
something strange was up: a scream, a hiss!

'I didn't kill the baby, Christ forgive!' – I think
that's what she yelled. The priest had raised

a Consecrated Host and prayed for mercy
for the abortionist. Then for the poor mother
'Why did the bishop give permission?' I'd
asked the priest. 'Why would he believe me,

A poor poet of sorts? And that orb!' Fr John
laughed in his nervous way and sighed.
'Apparently, Rosie Raddie was the niece.
She was his favourite child in the world'.
'Your mother and Rosie were best friends.
She was allowed to communicate with you'.

'It was a kind of Indulgence that still operated
in the old days – certainly into the Fifties'.
'The bishop may be this or may be that, but
he loves his family; loves the female voice'.
'He managed to persuade the local parish priest –
a stickler for Canon Law – to allow the exorcism'.

I never came across an orb again – never set foot
in the Kicking-Horse kitchen. Might have been a dream.
But Rosie I did see. Once, in a kind of dream:
Just along by Caugherty Brae, in moonlight.
Holy smoke: two attractive girls. Out for a walk.
Smoking. One was definitely Rosie.

The other the spitting-image of my mother!

Sliabh Mish

Whenever I see
Slemish disappear from view
I think of you.

These days it happens
quickly – my Lancia fairly
flies along the bypass –

once it was a slow affair,
a gradual slide into
the Antrim air,

a hill where youthful energy
allowed the picnic,
the faithful coat thrown down.

Like a brown tench slips
back to depth, her orange eyes
so cold and new,

Slemish disappears from view
and I think of you –
so transient but true.

ETHLENN

i

In a dream last-night
a dove-grey cloud
covered the moon's sickle.

Silence swallowed the rumbling
carriage up the hill –

beyond its windows swam
the black woods of Breen.

Looming out of the dusk,
like dandelions,
bubbles of oiled lamps,

heat lightnings,
red sky flames –

striving to light up
the houses of the poor.

In Ethlenn's father's house
the golden little spear
of a candle lit her hair,

a raspberry-coloured scarf,
little French books –

'Love is strong as death'
from his unmatching lips.

ii

In a dream last-night
no bitter vision to me
that woman's green eyes,

That she vanished into air
above an Antrim glen –

('People can love five times,
but still live on', he said).

I had watched her knock
thieves from the candle's stem
with a little teaspoon.

Was she caught herself against
some briar bush's barb –

that man's head,
smooth jackdaw?

Her face became the sea:
alive as whin gold,
her body shook for me.

I started up as her,
troops leaderless –

faint but hopeful
bright ships arrive.

III

Paradise

La Casa in Italia

for Nicola

'From where did this world come? Was it here for ever? There should be a history of this Italy, a history outside the framework of time, confining itself to what is changeless and eternal, in other words, mythology. This Italy has gone its way in darkness and silence, like the earth, in a series of recurrent seasons and recurrent misadventures. Every outside influence has broken over it like a wave, without leaving a trace' – *Carlo Levi*

i

In the upper room: Caruso;
Snow-flakes on the shutters.

Below the dark mountain: olives
and cheese-bread for breakfast.

A Cardinal had preached (and preached) …
Questo e il giorno che il fatto …

Until I understood Dante, and sang
O Signore, Signore nostro …

Till I was back in All Saints, Ballymena,
in the joy of Easter, in Bolignola.

ii

Gentiana! Maybe that was it –
the poitin of the Piceni!

Or it could have been the deep local red,
the clear limestone crystal of their white.

'There's a field', she said, 'without grass' –
not Bifana, mind you, the Epiphany witch that

still hung on the side of the house – but Bellina,
the image of my mother, busy cooking.

iii

'A room without doors' – she continued, 'a saint
without a name'. In Padua!

'Buona Pasqua', the elderly cousin said, 'the lamb
is almost ready'.

We Irish had journeyed into the mountains after
Easter Sunday morning mass in Loreto.

In that deep valley, in that warm house
in the Sibillini mountains, what joy!

iv

The snow fell suddenly that April day – we stood
out on the stone balcony in admiration.

Behind us, from a deep-throated fireplace,
limestone heat stones sent out Piceni shadows.

Checkerwise shadows on my mother's face
bounced off long thin logs laid from Frederico's hand.

Red and brown roof tiles whitened, walls
grew into the very roots of the mountain.

V

The hills above the house grew gaunt, scarred,
tremoring, tormenting – silenced too;

Resigned to their suffering, their feudal history.
Did Christ stop here? No contadino remain.

Bellina comes only at the weekends. Even
Nicola thinks with homesickness of his home!

vi

In Le Marche, on Easter Sunday,
in Bolignola, my mother would have danced.

I thought the fourteen of us were seated like
a scene in Thomas Hardy's *Wessex Tales,*

round the long table, more like a wedding
than a wake in Ballymacaldrick, Dunloy.

This was earthquake country – slopes above the house
scarred by erosion, their paths rutted.

'Jesus', I thought, 'we might stay here for ever,
hunting and climbing and skiing and walking the dogs'.

vii

Nicola escorted me on a short walk above the house –
the lamb was cooking nicely.

I hoped to see, or sense at least, a red deer or steppe horse –
Nicola said fallow deer, chamois and ibex once roamed here.

These days the Gentilis hunted in the forest around Sarnano
for wild pigs – not for their ancient roe deer.

Our spirits walked with us amongst the animals
of the Old Stone Age.

Snowflakes whitened rosemary, cistus broom –
lentisk, juniper, evergreen oak, phillyrea!

viii

I wanted to be here for ever, up and up,
to acacia, tree-heather.

I asked Nicola: 'Is there a path to the summits,
across these slopes of Mesozoic limestone?'

I was as it were 'day-dreaming' in Irish, the snow
barely touching these ancient spirits.

We returned for the first pastas,
for the lamb, and Irish whiskey.

Anna had arranged the giant Easter Eggs –
but dark and sweet wines were being decanted.

ix

The snow continued to fall, 'lying' as we say,
five or six inches but low on the snow poles

as we returned to Recanati along the mountain
roads. I thought of my three sons and only daughter –

and, strangely, of local flowers in the Corpus Christi
procession, in All Saints, in Ballymena.

Same Fire, Different Parish

visiting a church in Osimo, Italy

A fire burning far within a cave
attracted us in to a quiet gloom
while our offspring dandered on
to catch a dying sun –

we chose the inner gloom –
a church's sick-room for old Italians
praying their Rosary together
with an even older priest –

for that fire still burning
deep within our hearts,
that ancient faith, make us
less afraid of mortal death.

VIA FLAMINIA

The Trenitalia Ancona Express slows down
    between Apennine tunnels
and a quiet little valley appears
    to allow me to catch sight
of an old woman straddled side-saddle on a parapet.

She sits sideways on the ancient footbridge
    to ease her legs, to rest her black bag
along the limestone cobbles- or to look down
    into the mountain stream beneath her
swollen feet? The April sun glistens off her brow,

off the marching-legion sheaves across the bridge –
    yet she wonders only if she'll make it home:
Two hours from Rome, from the thousands tramping
    along the Corso: centurions, sentries, tourists,
Garibaldi, clerical students, Recanati's Leopardi

From my first-class carrozza ferroviaria seat I call out to her
    (did she turn her head a little?): Granny, Granny! –
lost in the sudden quickening of the train,
    of her first-born son; caught forever somewhere
in the thuddening of an Irish heart.

The Yellow Bird

for Sofia

I once saw a yellow bird
fly through the trees
above Sarnano, and knew then
she would escape the black hawk!

Her mountainy angels
followed her down to the cover
of the warm hills – the hawk a black dart
after her astonishing light.

Her beauty stunned the very air,
her movements genetic, yes, but
true to her being, borrowing
Heaven from the pure Sibillini sky.

I sensed then that this might be
my great gift from God
that she would save my soul.

Semper

for P.H.

That January –
snow was falling in the Troodos,
Emer throwing snowballs at their ghosts –
shadows that might have kept growing
white-scars, on tree-stems, on arched windows
at Downpatrick Cathedral, on beach-stones
of Rossknowlagh, of Ess-na-Larach!

Like sugar-cane boiling in a pan
white clouds mixed over Carey –

That January –
images of joy and love
filled snowy spaces in my heart.

THE IRISH QUARTER

for Laurentia

The sun drew his boat
over the Lough almost
below Cavehill; his thoughts
like rose blooms, gooseberries
that day, her birthday.

Every cloud welcome; Carrick
loved that warm rain: like
heaven, he said to himself
to be near home, near my children.

The sun left the Lough, high hopes
for a good haul of mackerel
as the light rain wet his forehead:
'What survives of us', he thought,
'but memory of an old road,
a green field, for her young heart'.

Conor and the Grogan

for Conor Michael McGuckian on his Christening Day

Goblins loving long sedgy grass,
during daylight in the Dunloy Bog
Grogan lay like a heavy log.

Though fond of making his drudging way,
that night he moved at a quicker pace
to Brackney, a speckly place.

Old Grogan lay his body down, stetched out
all along the chimney's length,
basking at the dying turf his hairy strength.

At the moth hour he appeared dead
but he overheard a noisy rant
as 'ceabh, ceibh', a fairy chant.

'A lock of his hair, he's asleep in his cot;
the travellers told us it's only one:
it be's a silver tooth from a second son!'

'*Anois ar theacht an tsamhradh*, true
we love the speckly grass, the truth,
but more than this we want his tooth!'

Now Grogan was low but desperately strong
and shook his fist as he rose from the fire:
'Touch that cradle and you'll feel my ire!'

Old Grogan held an ancient geis
so The Gentry flew across the floor
their golden carbad at the door.

'We're off to Gortateean they chanted:
Grogan would keep us til daylight
and then the glen would hold no flight!'

Wise Grogan drew a Loughgiel poitin;
and Conor slept with his silver tooth,
never ever guessing the goblin truth!

Grogan – a goblin (Antrim spelling).
Carbad – a small chariot.
Brackney is in Glenshesk.
Dunloy and Loughgiel are the home places of some of Conor's ancestors.
Ceabh agus ceibh refers to a lock of hair.
The Gentry are said by some to be Tuatha De Danaan from under Knocklayde.
Gortateean is a townland near Cushendall.

THE TRAVELLING PLAYERS

for Anew McMaster & Co.

That Cassius' feet were sore was deeply felt
as we approached crossroads at Carnlough Bay;
A big meal might do it ,might bring us back to life:
Five actors, four actresses from Belfast .

All along the way we rehearsed our play,
Friar Francis, a psycho-drama, an exposé
of religious tensions in ancient Irish strife.

Borrow the furniture ,the lackey said,
Lord Antrim will pay for all breakages.
No vulgar words concerning payment of course
but we knew Friar Francis could be staged at will.

No slight chance here of being adjudged and deemed
'Roges, Vaccaboundes and Sturdy Beggers',
we had walked for days along the route
of the Dalriada Stagecoach, assured
of safe passage, without robberies or harm.

Two furlongs beyond the Derry Arms
a rough-spoken doorknob of a thief
demanded all our goods and worldly chattels:
'If my father was a rogue, you clot,
I'll have you know he was jailed for it at Carrick
for less than murder of a dozen men,
so get you off or I'll have your very socks' –
at Cassius' words, and marvelling at his feet,
the fool took fright at such a desperate fellow.
And such a solid Players' Company.
I'd known Cassius once to lose his cool
over livery and break the peace and draw
his blade at Canterbury.

We'd been on our very heels these several months,
Othello and Polonius
worried about straitened financial circumstances.
But through the Antrim mist at noon appeared
a great Door and beyond a worthy Castle.
Sick of Mouthalles and Innes and Towne Halls,
we knew we'd found a true community.

The stone floor, the timber-framed wall,
the pitched cruck frame ceiling –
'maybe a hundred feet by thirty-three',
Aristotle thought, using his one good eye –
the changing area a veritable paradise
for the ladies , all deep mirrors and leaden glass
and perfumes everywhere and great lights;
Ah, we leapt high in the air for the play's sake.

Free food, safe accommodation,
a big audience flooding in:
I warned the players about the Queen Anne chairs,
the low ceiling that should be left unharmed.

On a big upper-end of hall dias,
Friar Francis suddenly appeared, the hush
awesome, and I felt that ancient thrill.
'The Plague is upon us', 'run for your lives', he cried,
and the poor people rose to suck in their breath and flee.
'Not even the Famine touched us', Lord Antrim upspake,
'so many golden salmon flourished in
the strong and goodly water of Glenarm'.

At this, of course, our little play went on,
and even Cassius found a local wench
to knit him woollen socks for love's sake!

EOCHAIDH

(Ulster Archaeological Society found Fir Bolg Burial Urns at Greenan, nr. Ballycastle, Co. Antrim)

Here we be:
Here my people lie;
Calm, islanded, native.

That were beautiful once
now gardens of wild garlic,
mosses, lichens and old mushrooms.

Like our mother's eyes,
now woodsmoke,
the stitches of the glen.

Virga

for P.J. Leahy, RIP

Ireland, 2038 A.D.
Recording the temptation of Brother O'Flynn

i. his church

Last abbot on the island –
his dear friend –
allowed him then in that old age
to cut a hazel wand from the wood-glen
near The Tower
to live – at least in his own mind –
'secundam regulam beati Benedicti'.

This vast solitude – a little isolated valley
in bits and pieces of oak and ash –
would be his church: without side-lighting,
he said to himself, sunbeams would be truly
striking at its eastern end; narrow lancet
windows in side-walls of basalt stone –
in truth natural gaps in the hazel-wood –
a polygonal apse with three double lancets
opposing a moderate rose window,
would remind him of Sénanque.

ii his struggle

Leaning on his spade –
that potato-rig half dug –
Brian saw how visitors
might gain cloister access
by a north portal, its plain
tympanum, rolled arches,
simple colonettes.

A cold wind cut his heart
like a turnip; big veins rose
on the back of his hand:
he couldn't pray.

He had thought St Anthony might find
him one more May-time prayer
for one more year of mortal life,
or even send his friend Dermot
to read him slowly *'as na Ceithre Soisceail'*.

Isn't this a little haven, the Darkman said;
that pain a mere niggle for such a fine boyo
and only a leftover from fucking sons, maids,
hoors, bastards, nuns, dogs sheep –
you oul shite, your cock withered;
whatever you want you shall have:
gold in your pocket, not that shit shovel;
you're an evil creature, full of lust and pride –
(the Darkman frothed at the mouth) –
barren, dried up like the seeds you sieve
in your hand; maybe I'll find you
that maid for sex ...

iii assistance

You're a right bollocks, Brian –
his favourite saint at the spade –
would I forget you?
say 'Penance' out loud,
'by God and His Holy Mother'.

iv prayer

'Oh God of old
that my father loved

drag me up from this
terrible loneliness'.

v penance

Brian could hear sighs
and moans from Purgatory.
His ears more tuned to prayers
above Gregorian Chant;
Then his favourite saint again:
The Virga in his grasp, the flying thoughts
of all the Celtic Peoples through his mind.

vi his garden

Brian grew herbs and dreamt
they were blown by Providence
from MacDara's island, off Galway:
'Enula campana reddit praecordia sana',
were the words he heard;
in his kitchen garden he nurtured
the Elecampane
that ancient Irish monks thought magical.

LUCINA

for Julia

They say I am fearful
I sleep with my eyes open
but I can tell you I will be the last to go.

They call it 'Cutting the Hare'
tiny 'beasts' scamper out and away
as the field of corn is reduced in size.

I am left now among the last stalks
I am a solitary being after all
but I might shoot out like the moon behind a cloud.

They will say I gave myself up
that I could have escaped
that I would rather jump into a fire.

They can't claim it's March Madness
this silver-yellow sun will soon rise
and I will with it to see my grandmother on the moon:
the last to run!

The Blue Distance is Delirious

for Henry McAuley

Winds from off Slemish
sharpen here
on the sandstone of The Pillars.

Above the Braid Valley
tall trees guard the graves
of my family.
As for a breath of air from Deerfin
after the town, my mother
would hasten up the brae:

The blue is so blue here
she never minded the sighing
of the sallies along Woodside.

My mother could hear his voice
over the corncracked mosses
long after he passed.

Her father's voice was sweet
as buttermilk to her, soft and low,
like a cloud making music.

She couldn't forget her remembering
of time, her subsistence
on the charity of Protestant neighbours.

The Fourth Bell

High above the Braid
yon bell
at Deerfin, Kate's Hill, Caugherty.

Not the footprint
of a helicopter on my house alarm;
an Irish bell, in caves,
over cemeteries, rock-ledges,
Crebilly, Dunnyvadden, Kildoney.

Above myself
and in my head, my city psion:
Cavehill, McCracken lives!

Through seven years
four families, Emerian tears,
for Cothraige;
through paths of Killyfluigh
for Milcho-ua-Buain.

On Ascemsion Thursday afternoon,
after the Battle of Ballymena,
on John O'Hara's farm,
on Boydstown Rock,
for The Boys Frae The Braid.

High above us
yon square bell
still in Deerfin
Dun-na-Feinne
Kate's Hill
Caugherty!

PARADISE

Quando corpus morietur,
Fac ut animae donetur
Paradisi gloria – Rossini

i

My mother's people kept two caves
near Deerfin
their floors paved in Precepts of
the Old Faith.
Their walls lined with ancient
Irish prayers
that had the ears of Paradise.

My ancestors had a Mass-Rock
at Boydstown, later
a chapel at Crebilly; nearby
a schoolhouse that echoed to Master
Loy's Old Catechism.
My parents were married there;
Their sins shriven.

ii

Now, four black stones of Antrim basalt
mark the old chapel amidst a field
of family names: McAuleys, Raddies,
Agnews, Vaughans. The dust from cloths
that lined the altar rails; the dust from flowers
that welcomed Easter, lies buried here.
Walk gently past the Calvary, still strong.

iii

Once I found the Dunnyvadden Rath,
its warm shield of hazel. And near the
Mass-Rock at Boydstown, a basalt rose.
Now the old schoolhouse no longer had
its little iron gate my mother might have touched,
might have left open for me.

Once, above the rath,
its warm shield of hazel,
home to the basalty rose,
you and I made love.
We raised the mould from round
the stone and bade it speak
of other days.
We rubbed the mould
from round the stone
lest we forget
how well it's kept.

About the Author

John McGuckian was born in Ballymena, Co. Antrim. At Queen's University, Belfast he studied geography under the inspiration of Etsy Evans and was a Full Blue in Association Football. He is a MA graduate of Creative Writing at the Seamus Heaney Centre for Poetry in Belfast. He has read at the International Poetry Festival, Visby, in Sweden; at the John Hewitt Spring School, Carnlough, and at the Summer School of the Seamus Heaney Centre. His first collection, *Talking with my Brother*, was published in 2002 by Summer Palace Press. His current interests are in the study of sixteenth century Italian poetry – especially that of Giacomo Leopardi of Recanati – and in supporting Ballymena United FC. His most recent publication is *Star and Sparrow Rest* (Summer Palace Press, 2008).